D0734685

Plain
Air

UNIVERSITY OF CENTRAL FLORIDA
Contemporary Poetry Series

George Bogin, *In a Surf of Strangers*
Van K. Brock, *The Hard Essential Landscape*
Gerald Duff, *Calling Collect*
Malcolm Glass, *Bone Love*
Susan Hartman, *Dumb Show*
Lola Haskins, *Planting the Children*
Hannah Kahn, *Time, Wait*
David Posner, *The Sandpipers*
Nicholas Rinaldi, *We Have Lost Our Fathers*
Robert Siegel, *In a Pig's Eye*
Edmund Skellings, *Face Value*
Edmund Skellings, *Heart Attacks*

Plain
Air

Poems by

Michael McFee

A University of Central Florida Book
University Presses of Florida
Orlando

Acknowledgments

Thanks go to these publications for first printing these poems:

American Poetry Review: Dvořák in the Open Air
The Archive: Winter Suite
Bellingham Review: The Mockingbird,
Hay Fever, Amoretti
Carolina Quarterly: Ceremonial, Mixed Blessings
Columbia: A Magazine of Poetry and Prose:
The Birdbath
Georgia Review: The Okra Flower
Hollins Critic: Buster Keaton
Kansas Quarterly: Twice in the Same Place
Massachusetts Review: Silo Letter in the Dead of a
Warm Winter
The Nation: Visiting Cape Hatteras
New North Carolina Poetry: The Eighties: Homing
No Business Poems: Gilbert White and the Bobwhite,
Summer Modes, Plain Air
Poetry Now: Retirement
The Small Farm: Pisgah Bald
Southern Poetry Review: Holiday Around the House,
On the Porch
Western Humanities Review: Bean Arbor,
At Play

Contents

III

To B.

Wo du, Engel, bist,
    ist Lieb und Güte,
Wo du bist, Natur.

DIRECTIONS

Come by the fast road as far as the river
    with a funny name. Turn left over
the shoal bridge—it will have been repaired
    since that recurrent nightmare.
Pass the valley school, standard fortress of brick,
    and the transforming power lake.
You will come to one stoplight, local joke, facing
    a mostly vacant volunteer plaza—
fire department, branch library, P.O. Turn right,
    away from the veneer of lights.
When you face a choice at the triple fork, follow
    the leftmost tine, toward that low
mountain; and when you buck across the sunken asphalt
    patch that looks like Africa,
bear left again, just past the weed-cracked gas
    station. After the underpass
the road gets narrow, convoluted—quick climb and fall,
    gravel or trash scattered in all
the worst turns—before it unexpectedly yields
    to countryside. Look for a field
spread to the left, a bungalow pinning its far corner:
    home at last. Park in the yard.
If I'm not on the porch, leave your bags on the lawn,
    come inside and lie down on
the ready bed for a while. If daylight grows lean
    and still I haven't been seen,
go out the back, downslope, to the old logging trail,
    a star-lost lovers' lane. You will

enter a cedar plantation, the steady rumor of creek.
   And the closer to it you get,
the more familiar everything feels, until you know,
   paused on the crossing stone,
that I have been watching you all along.

I

THE OKRA FLOWER

I stood in a ripe twilight
meaning to think about the mountains,
their brilliant hem all around,

but thought instead, I do not want
to die here, away from home, away
from her as she goes to the garden
to gather in this long light,
as she breathes the tang of tomatoes
and feels her forearms prickle
when she stretches to cut the okra.

I remembered how the okra flower
would be folded for the night,
how it held in itself the colors
of her face better than any picture,
the moon of her skin,
the rich purse of her lips.

I thought, when I get home again
I will stand at the kitchen window
and watch her stitch up the beans,
and a kind of healing will begin,
until the days ripen like a row
of vegetables on the bright sill,

until I can walk in the garden
on an early September afternoon
and look deep into the okra flower
without smell, without a freckle,
and not think of her, not her.

BEAN ARBOR

Mind spilled from its hard-won hammock,
he pauses at the mouth of this green tunnel,

then enters. Beans dangle just overhead
and at either side, supple stalactites.

Suddenly chilled, he pockets his hands and paces,
trying to forget the call that drove him here.

The light inside is baffled so handsomely,
he wishes the vines could cover him too.

When he picks a bean and snaps it in two,
he wants to remember some pantry's plenty.

He wants to believe that this is his bower,
that if he walked out the arbor's other end

instead of returning on himself, he would come out
in the clearing by the woods where the thrush

coils the dark air into tendrils of song
changed somehow, a new man in a garden.

THE BIRDBATH

In broccoli-light
everything is a version of itself
about to be dissolved,
like the cloudy limbs and sky
suspended in the birdbath.

Then is the time
to wade into that light
which looks so shallow, feels so deep,
and clean the stone
until the water holds no stain.

As the rest of day
compacts to this lens, a slim
reservoir of light,
it's hard to see my other self
bowed over the world's one offering,

but it's enough, soon
after, as I wait for a late bird
to breast the surface
before splintering my equilibrium
into utter darkness,

to think how,
on a sheer winter morning,
I will come to slide night's island
out of the stone bath
intact, a tablet of light on the lawn.

THE MOCKINGBIRD

Mimus polyglottos

In my dream, a bird began to sing
or I began to dream so that the song
would be part of a dream.

                      It woke me up.
The bird kept singing though the song had changed
and changed again before I reached the door.

I stepped onto the porch, and then the bird
began to broadcast seeds of song again.
I padded down the sidewalk toward the tree
which spoke so many tongues into the dark
or spoke the same phrase many different ways,
as if the breathless bird's recitative
translated the hidden tap of speech,
that password nested in each bird's name
then scattered in songs of generation.

I found the tree but couldn't break the code.
I caught some jokes—a black be*cause*, be*cause*,
the piercing laughter of the Lord God Bird—
and thought, if only I could rise like this
from the jealous bed of that other sleep,
I wouldn't mind returning as this bird

pouring through his pentecostal throat
some local versions of the lofty Song,
mysterious, but familiar to all.

The houses' doorbells glowed like little moons
about to fade. The polyglot fell quiet.
Soon tires would sing along the empty street
and birds rehearse their bright stitches of song,
swung like a patchwork in the sleepy air.

WINTER SUITE

1. *Snowbirds*

Juncos do a snow dance
between flurries, saltant,
clog, heel and toe, stamping
erratic patterns under
the food tree: for encore,
they snap into the high
lighted branches, a perfect
mirror of each snow limb.

2. *Cotillion*

Stately as a southern belle
in the bald room of winter,
the glossy magnolia gathers
a court of birds in her skirt,

choking the air with chatter
thick as memories of the smell
of her luscious candles
in summer's open window.

~ 11

3. *Blizzard*

Birds, snowblown into storm
    windows, must wish they didn't have
    to worry about wingbeat or angles
of approach or turbulence
    at takeoff ruffling their evolution
    into some stylish line: especially
the lipsticked cardinal
    chides the gravity filling her like
    the snow egg in last year's nest.

HOLIDAY AROUND THE HOUSE

Simply astonishing, the scripture
in a common yard, the blood
of Christ barely-born and -alive
lachrymal on the holly and dogwood,

or those local theophanies
of pyracantha, burning
since Moses learned his magic
from God on Horeb, hand
and staff and berry-red water.

And that mistletoe kissing
your lintel: do you think Druids
dressed Stonehenge at the solstice
just to buss and flirt
under its pale moons?

Imagine the myth
woven into a wreath's long vowel:

"When Melchior offered his frankincense,
the Baby cried and would not be pacified
until Mary plucked a sweet gumball
for him to handle, which is a natural
thurible, and which is why it appears
in the rafters of the gum at Advent-tide."

"After the royal court and heavenly host
a pine tree by the Via Exodus
dropped its last cone as a farewell gift
for the Child. Joseph picked it up, and smiled.
'When the shady world goes gray and naked,
you shall be wrapped in living fur, and jewels
shall petal on your limbs like perching birds,
and myrrh shall sweetly bead from every pore
even after shivered into timber,
because you gave out of your poverty.' "

*

Wee hours: the immaculate time
of miracle. You stretch outside
and blow your Santa's beard of breath
toward the skinny chimney.

Stars spangle the sky like frost.
Later, you will wake dreaming
they crystallize right over your house
with the fearful gleam of gospel.

SILO LETTER IN THE DEAD OF A
WARM WINTER

Silo: almost a greeting, or a goodbye, hi,
hello, so long, aloha, all in one: *silo,* Steve,
after so long, little to tell. Still no snow's
my main plaint: what's winter without weather?
(How's that for a Swinburnian hibernian line?)
Lately my mind's been turning, windmillish
tilting in the Piedmont, seriously, to silos:
a sevenfold interpretation, in fact, to pass
the time while internally combusting with the wife
here and there, a Neo-Agrarian, Demi-Southern
Digression in the Modern Kind. To wit:

1. *Architectural*

Somewhere, I swear, old Walt Gropius, dean
(so to speak) of the boxy Bauhaus, wrote: "Silos
are the unnoticed majesty of American architecture,"
one of those impressively unlikely aphorisms
I always relished but never believed. Well, one day
last fall, in *(sic)* transit *(gloria)*, sun setting
across a field combed with corn or tobacco,
farm cutout-plain on the horizon, I comprehended,
like with those photos of Chartres across a pasture
outside town: epiphany on state road one thousand

and something. It was then I realized how bliss-
fully ignorant farmers had translated millenia
of architectural history into a feed pit,
campanile to the barn's cathedral, classical
as a tin column, even domed and sectioned:
what a hybrid to hang (*true* American Gothic!)
Angus-like on the sign at the drive's mouth!

2. *Astronomical*

Simply that a dry and drafty silo
makes a stellar observatory for chickens.

3. *Etymological*

Root of silence. (Forget the *OED.*) Indo-
European *silo-*, suffixed (stative) form
*sil-e in Latin *silere*, to be silent.
Ergo *silo* = "I am silent," "I am ceasing,"
silebo = "I shall be still as cows on a hill
chewing their quiet redundant cud,
who trot toward the dark lighthouse
when silence rises with dew on the grass."

4. *Literal*

Best of all is the full balance of vowels,
high/low, the assonant teeth, the liquid
tongue, or the rich little anagrams
of *oils, soil, lois,* or the exotic company
in the dictionary, *silex, silique, silk,*
silva, unutterably lovely *silence.* (See 3.)

5. *Military*

Missilo? Somehow I can't imagine a silo
outside Rapid City wired and timed to rise,
fire, zip globewise, and pop Basil's bulbs.
But NADS assures me South Dakota could
prickle with missiles in a minute, on attack.

6. *Sexual*

(North American Defense System, that is, though
I imagine this link isn't imaginary, this
coincidence coincidental: testy nads, storage
for the phallic silo, obligatory Freudianism—
"built as if each erection were the last." No go.)

7. *Theological*

Bet you were expecting the pool of Siloam,
a brilliant link between Jesus' muddy miracle
and Georgia's clay, or an eschatological exposition
of the SilAge (also known as the Auto Age), the foolish
age in which we live and may well die: but no.
As before, a simple barnyard gloss, on the trinity
in the unity of silo: *fodder, sun,* and *holy goats.*

—Amen? Ah well: not a bad way to sidle up
to Swift, to saddle up the hack. Let me know
what you think of this madness. —And *silo.*

II

AT PLAY

Dreaming of diamonds and elegant courts
buffed so bright the lights in them blind
or fields trimmed and laddered with lime,
the boy sprints into the yard's weedy arena
and pulls a seasoned ball from the bushes.

Alone, he plays catch with gravity, shagging
the steep curves till his palms glow, inventing
a godlike defense, invisible, everywhere,
through which he must whirl and fall and rise
to salvation in the eyes of the faithful
in the final desperate seconds of each game.

From a window across the faulty street, a man
watches the boy hail the roof until his mother
storms the front door and orders him away.

The man remembers memorizing whole leagues
and lineups against the boredom of bitter
afternoons like these, how all that mattered
then was a store of chatter and averages,
how days could shrink to a single countdown
and shout, how life was held in the red stitch
of an old hide or the spin of a familiar bladder
balanced in the air, still pebbled and striped
like the globe of a world perfectly made
which would never stop turning or sink or burst.

ON THE PORCH

A place between—inside and out, daylight
and darkness, gossip's loose tongue
and groove of sleep. Around sunset, stomachs
sag heavy as the cane-bottom chairs
while ample rumps hug the thin banister,
every spine slumped in that familiar lull
of insects, anecdotes, and cigarettes.

If the boy could come back in fifteen years,
fresh-schooled and literary, he might
call it *visor for the memory,* and write:

"I remember this porch when I was only five,
mounting the rail like a dime ride
at the Park and, without a wooden neck
to press against, falling headfirst
onto the only stone of any dimension
in the entire block. Later, the collarbone
whole, I bolted down the front hall, sprung
the screen, tripped at the top of the stoop
and sailed away, folding my foolish arm
like a wing under me and snapping it
clean as a wishbone after Sunday dinner
when I hit the cracked concrete walk.

"And why I never fell from the steep roof
during cherry-picking time is a miracle,
when I crawled headlong out the attic window
and down into the sweet white branches,
beating the birds away, slipping
on rotten fruit and shingles,
stretched beyond my mother's endurance
as she leaned, pale and arthritic,
against the woodpecked trunk below.

"I remember this, with its white pillars,
narthex to the temple of my life,
holy to me as Herbert's Church-Porch."

If the rest of the family could hear him
they'd cough, and hawk, and watch the street
for some relief, some lame hound or truck
bucking down the hill, some excuse to snort
and spit and stir, some reason to retreat
to the plain talk of hall and parlor.

CEREMONIAL

To save the terminal elm, crusted
with a leprous patina, circle it
like a millenial imagination of bark,
treading its audible well of shadow
until some limb will suffer you to climb
childlike to the still green crown,
to carry down in your own soft skeleton
the blight that lightens this tree
and feel the brittle lacery of leaves
returning from their spiritual season
perfect as a child's rendering.

—But if vision fails,
if birds flirting or squirrels
branching or a half-imagined breeze
brings untimely abscission, restore
at least the memory of elm, inventing
a new letter, mid-alphabet, for it,
or pulping its stubborn heart of wood
into a heavy, deckled ream.

—And if vision wholly fails,
have the old shade laid to rest,
climb to the marginal roof, scoop
some seedlings from the gutter's sediment
and plant them in a clear glass on the sill
until their slight roots can sustain
one century, tree and bright child
and hope of a harder grain and ornament.

TWICE IN THE SAME PLACE

I prowl the summer dusk with my niece, palming
jars full of a different kind of lightning.
When I was her age, these local air raids
were less cautious—missing wings, fingers
luminescent as skeletons, containers shaken
to a dull lantern-glow and chemical stench.

Silly with the signals filling her yard, Stephanie
orders me to catch them quick before the boys do.

We circle in the street waiting for the night
to pulse, but before long the only code
is the ricochet of crickets and tree insects.
Stephanie says it's because the fireflies
have all risen to become stars. I tell her
news travels like lightning among the Lampyridae.

Liberation is a disappointment. Some bugs
blink into the bushes, a few stick to the jar:
she beats the bottom like a ketchup bottle. Most
glow in the grass at our feet like cigarettes
flipped away. When she screws the lid back on
the sound threads every tree in the neighborhood.

"It's OK," I say, "fireflies have large families."
Already she moves through the dew to her mother.

ORDER OF BAPTISM

Heavy curtains part above the choir
on this proscenium of paradise:
a blue arboretum of palms, cedars,
every Biblical bush; empty bulrushes,
the promised river bending out of sight,
this baptismal pool its headwaters.
A flock of clouds, placid and orderly
in soft light, perspective-perfect, attends
the possibility of word from heaven.

Has there ever been such a mild scene?

When the preacher wades in, Baptist-deep,
and the nervous children, as worried
about their robes as any salvation,
disappear behind the witnessing glass
to rise wetter than snow, who can keep
the mind from wanting to lift up and sail,
like cast-out sin, through that holy window
into a landscape, exotic, serene,
where no human's being can ruin it?

BUSTER KEATON

Into the frenzy of falling bodies
and chaos of pastry, apollonian
and sober even as an infant,
he came, just as decades later
he would calmly step into a frame
and never leave. In the curious
oracle of his face, distant and mute
and abstracted perfect as statuary,
the lesson of his life could be seen:

Patience. Be humble. Believe in grace
and miracles of our own foolish making.
Words are mostly waste. Laughter,
like love, is a rigorous discipline.
Think slow. Act fast. Persevere.

After Hollywood's sacred grove
has babbled, blushed, and scattered,
his image quietly endures, surviving
even when the small boat of his career
launches bottomward like an anchor,
his body stubborn as a lonely buoy
fixed on the horizon, until he sinks
(soon to return, grave-faced) beneath
his flat hat floating on the water.

Or angled over some final tombstone:
the god of light, poetry, and movies
still laughs at that one, Buster.

WRITTEN IN SOUND AND LIGHT

Thumbing the records at the library,
like specimens at a mineral museum,
a rack of cold cuts of obsidian
or some petrified sections from the trunk
of that tremendous mulberry called Music,
I pause, involuntarily, over
the Brahms F-minor piano quintet
with Rudolph Serkin and the Budapest
"performing together for the first time"—
an unremarkable jacket design,
five old men in an old photograph—
because I catch you beaming out at me,

not as I might at the millenium
over your likeness in the old yearbook
and nod, nostalgic, "That's him, by God,"
but as if I had made a brassy wish
to open one window on the future
and was not shown myself, but only you
sitting in a garden's cultured shade
with four harmonious ambassadors,
flourishing your memorable smile
till every feature crinkles with pleasure,
even the burnished skin of your head
surrounded by its white horseshoe of hair.

So I checked out the record and went home
and listened, as well as I could manage
over warps and years of graffiti,
to the billows of Brahms' sublime scherzo
straining to transcend its instruments
("Don't that sound like rats running up stairs,"
the secretary would say, changing stations)
as excavated by my dim stylus
performing the archaeology of sound
written as on a single coil of hair
barberpoling toward the label's drain,
the death of concerto and symphony,
the illegible glide into silence,

and I scrutinized the text of light
written on the sleeve, the photograph
translating me into another time
remote as the music's stuttering pulse,
where figures that should be familiar
as a certain melody or face or name
fade instead like brittle images
beyond sight or hearing, obsolete,
where you sit in a funereal suit
with a brilliant silk tie disappearing
like a slice of sky into your hands,
folded, but about to burst into sound.

RETIREMENT

When you turn the familiar corner and find
some schoolkids kneedeep in a lot of pumpkins,
      it is hard to keep driving.

You want to idle at the curb and watch them
wade through this treeless windfall,
      looking for the class lantern.

When a little boy hoists a big one to his chest,
don't think, as I might, that he is like
      Atlas wobbling under the globe

of his life, as if anyone could hold, once
but long ago, the impossible burden of his time,
      so strangely brilliant and cut off.

Think instead of the sweet pie we will eat,
of the toothy likeness we will carve and light,
      of your hands still harvest-ruddy.

HOMING

The sky seems closer, the room more cluttered,
the local foliage more dense and ridiculous
than before, when this was all the world
we knew. Now the instinct is centrifugal,
out and away from the inevitable whine
of television, children, idle contradictions.
Yet guilt still remains, the imperative to honor,
the undertow of origin. At home, though not
at home: that ancestral row of portraits
windowing the wall with coffin-black frames
must come down, to be stacked in the attic,
the tiny wire nails in our hammer's claw
leaving holes in the sheet rock as clean
as the pattern on our parents' memory.

MIXED BLESSINGS

1.

Most people, spent on a living,
can't afford the luxury of looking
at what most surrounds them.
How do you see what's always there?

And so we drive my parents,
who have never lived anywhere else,
out to see the mountains again.

2.

Every road is an argument.
My folks, spoiled by the smooth talk
of superhighways, the presumption
of an open cut, grow restless
with the old-fashioned decorum
of this back road, its progress
by insinuation, the natural
reasoning of creek or cowpath
along the line of least resistance:

slow to address the ridge,
a few anecdotal doodles, then
into its seasick rhythm, weaving

up and forth, back and down, a spring
recoiled on itself, a blacksnake
whiplashing out of sight, the drunk
dead end of the alphabet, u's and v's
and w's and z's so elbowed and ingrown
we cross ourselves coming back—

then suddenly it relaxes
into valley, a minute
of rectitude and bottomland,
before disappearing up the next rise
like a spiral of smoke.

3.

And every trip is finally
a detour into the past. How many
eternal Sunday afternoons
did we glide the high Parkway
for my father's sake, descending
with tourists to Cherokee
or climbing to Devil's Courthouse
where Mother, who hates heights,
shouted us back from the cliff-edge?

I liked looking at souvenirs
but not the mountains: they were
just another fact of landscape
to be crayoned into school drawings
like geometric trees or houses,

a purple sawtooth horizon line
with sun always wedged into gap
like (now I know) a gingko leaf,
rays blazoned across the sky
bold as on the library's bookplate
with its holy words and seal,
Levavi oculos meos in montes.

When do children and parents
trade places? Today I drive
and Dad reads signs, naps,
hums, demands Coke and bathrooms.
Mother's guts are knotted as the road.

4.

Bent to the map, no one guessed
the intestinal folds of this route.
It's a matter of translation,
of imagining the map a model,
earth's braille, blister of ridge
and scar of gap, then reading
its relief by fingertip the way
the wind does, memorizing ranges
until the polished peaks glow bald,
Mt. Mitchell worried to a callus.

To feel with your eyes—that
is vision, the forms vernacular
at last, the world made flesh.

5.

But even from Prospect Ridge—
high on the Divide, the last
judgment of the elements, where
hindsight and future fall away
from your feet like so much rain—
nothing is seen only for itself:

staring at that vacant range
gradually a shape emerges
like some holy face from a cloud,
a girl sleeping on her side,
the convolutions of the crest
her contours lipped by light
after a remembered picnic,
adolescent on a blanket . . .

then, like a simple word gone
foreign under scrutiny, it dissolves
into that deep cleavage of leaves
piled in the backlot last fall,
which seized me late one afternoon

with such inarticulate longing
I thought I'd weep over my rake.

The least glance is mixed
with history, like a shout
rebounding from below as echo,
whole yet wholly transformed.
How easily the eye's deflected,
the mind's eye, the heart's!
Shivering at the shoulder,
a primary school of hills below
like sediment on the heavenly floor,
my parents drift apart to other
blue ridges, great wars, loves,
lives wasted on work or family.
I remember Poor Richard's half-
truth: *Men meet, mountains never.*

6.

After suffering enough hairpins
to permanent Medusa, after
dozens of gapfoot towns
with Manichean cattle
all grazing compass-true
on the pasture's stiff pitch
and file cabinets of bees
beside trailers with vast antennae
straining to pull the outside in,
perched on a block and a prayer,

I stop for directions. We land
at this toolshed of a church
in a red sea of clay and planks.
Inside, as if from another century,
a "true fresco," "The Lord's Supper."
Christ is so muted, his expression
so ambiguous, my father has to ask
which one Jesus is. "I think
the one looking toward that dog
asleep at the foot of the stairs."
The disciples gab as usual, Judas
slinking away, his empty stool
the seat and focus of the scene.
From the rafters, a ray-like shroud
begins its sinister descent toward
the distracted Lord, the window
behind him a splendent blank.

At the evergreen sister church,
two frames from his deep daydream.
"St. John the Baptist," brawny
and bronzed in the wilderness,
raises hand and angles staff
to sweep home another point
to another band of hypocrites,
but his eyes betray him:
instead of piercing the quick
with fierce prophetic glint,
they fade to introspective haze,

remote and yet intimate
as the surrounding mountains.

"Mary Great with Child," pregnant
patron of this mission, stands
barefoot in a barren land.
With her right hand she cradles
the scandal visible in her belly;
the other, uplifted in a kind
of casual absolution, a farewell
to the buried life, indicates
an eclipse in the bruised sky
that mirrors her own mystery.
Like the others, she seems lost
in thought, almost bemused, about
the mixed blessings of her state.

7.

Bored with iconography,
my parents smoke outside.
So we take the Parkway back,

and it happens again, as before:
a mile in the sky, we climb into
the belly of a leviathan cloud
making its way to open valley
on the ridge's yonder side.

What a load of glory left behind,
what mantles on the laurels!
And the higher our car crawls
the more brilliant and silent
everything becomes, until we stop,
alone at the heart of light.

Is this how we'd have heaven?
I open the door, and fog
floods the car: Dad cracks his
and it passes through us
like we aren't even there,
a party of ghosts, erased,
beyond sense, pure element.
Could grace be so neutral,
so numb and suffocating?

I'll take my vision fallen
below the tonsure of cloudline,
where real tires whimper on
a real shoulder, where families
can carve their hard life out
of the foothills and still care
though shin-splinted by curves
and swaybacked with foolish burdens,
where the sublime is only a promise
banked at the far edge of sight
as the mountains' high tide
watersheds light into a blue rainbow.

III

DVOŘÁK IN THE OPEN AIR

There were men with blue tattoos
and wives with ham-fat arms and dogs
with metronomic tails and tongues
all sweating in the sun and soaking
up the notes, the sound alive in chins
and bright in cheeks and knees and shoulders,
felt even by restless buttocks and kids,
all sleepy as a treble clef and all
imagining the long pale fingers
and perfect feet of the philharmonic.

JUST

The world angling
for me—the jays' spooky two-tone
notes quivering as if underwater,
          the felt screen of
heat as I lean out the window
to fix them, the copper-colored
          leaf swooping toward
my face, then banking and climbing
away—a moth! I thought it was
          just the sickly elm
dropping more money in the fountain
that surrounds it, lucid even in
          the thick of summer.

          —So I volley a few
whistles with the jaywalking birds.

HAY FEVER

Myth's one way of talking around
this seasonal fallout of the trees—
puddles scummed with Midas-touch
like the river below the paper mills,
gold dust squalling from the pines
faster than Zeus after another wife,
boards on the porch caulked sulfurous
as if St. Rock had fallen on our stoop
and pulverized his halo's brittle leaf
or the Treasure of the Sierra Madre
had finally blown up from Mexico
on the gale of Huston's last laugh.

—But myth's no comfort for your nose
as you lie in bed, cross and pollinated,
except perhaps as soporific, say,
Jesus sawing golden planks for Joseph
or God chalking a new commandment
over and over, until the air dances
with particles radiant as ether.
And if you should ask about oxygen
or the meaning of the words, the dust
will lift off the floor soft as fog
and wrap you in a sleep beyond breathing.

THE NATURALIST'S DAYDREAM

Euonymus americanus *is a wild*
shrub commonly known as the "straw-
berry bush" or "hearts a-bustin'."

If she were here, I'd backslide off the path
down to this bush, and call, Hey, come look.
She'd pick a prudent route as I study
the spiny heart that splits itself open,
petals back to show scarlet chamber-beads
dangling for one sharp beak or breeze.

What will I tell her when she arrives,
maple-flushed, leaf-charged, out of temper?
Some soothing parable of the Sacred Heart?
How my wildflowering heart swells too
with love, to the very bursting point?
Or that—less lie—it's not exactly love
that makes our swung hearts, like this plant,
bare bloody secrets, squeeze life into seed,
but some need without a good name, a passion
that bears peculiar fruit, both sour and sweet?

Look here, I say: Hearts a-bustin' with love.
I scatter a few berries with my fingernail

and crush some others on my thumb to sniff.
I move to slip the last one in my mouth—
she grabs me by the wrist and says, Wait.
The confederacy of fog begins to rise.

AMORETTI

1. *Invocation*

Come scratch my back, baby, I mean
    really nail it between the blades!
Let your fingers shinny down my spine
    and stir the topsoil down in the valley,
Come scout out the faults and folds
    embossed along this ridge of rib—

No, I mean it, *really* bulldoze, baby,
    rearrange the landscape if you have to,
From cervix to coccyx, from stubborn Dan
    to Beersheba, from Murphy to Manteo:
Chainsaw the lumbar! raise up the sacrum!
    horse around my ilium for a while—

O holy and flexible phalanx, O "thin,
    horny, transparent plates covering
The dorsal surface of the tip of each
    finger," I worship your harrowing!
All ten crisp crescents, a full moon
    in each white hand, cool as a crater,

I praise you! The savage itch (poor
    me) has been soothed indeed,
The evil spirits are appeased and I am

purring (O onomatopoeia!) like a cat,
There is balm in Gilead and salvation
in the diligent palm of my love.

2. *Tune-Up*

Baby, the way you
unwind from the rocking
chair, recovering chest
     and balancing abutment
with one breath, frankly
makes my valves flutter.

3. *Son Bain d'Hiver*

Never a goose with flesh so stippled
as when you shiver into the coffin
cold as our original mold,

never an Easter lily risen from snow
with so luminous a tongue.

Never a shell held so siren an ocean
or pearly goddess scalloped from the foam,

never marble so quick as this
I shock with the raw brand of my hands.

4. *The Importance of Being Earnest*

Sometimes when I lie with you, love,
recumbent or semi-so, especially
if on my sinister side, my nether arm
intervenes like something uninvited
or redundant, vestigial as an appendix.

5. *Midwinter Night's Dream*

I saw you above in a white
union suit, hanging half out
of the library's stern windows,
whooping and singing tarzannas

till a cumulonimbus shingle
of snow thundered down
from the gray slate, suspended
loud as a waterfall's curtain

between me and the bright world.
When I stretch for sanctuary,
quiet and dry, I wake to my hand
whole on your ribs' radiator.

6. *Baroque Goldenrod*

Lightning in allegro
   strokes across the static night:
then the contrapuntal grumble
   of thunder and your *schnauzetrompete*
bubbling in allergo.

7. *In the Air*

Never lackluster with you
here, dear, pheromones
swirling around the house
in delicious systems, yeast,
shampoo, fishy musk,

smells almost visibly dense:

right now my nostrils feast
after a flat midmorning,
tickled silly by your sweet
wet armload of laundry
and fine features of sweat!

8. *Petite Gigue*

When, bent to the furious stove,
you suddenly furl your skirt
at half-mast and spin around
the kitchen smiting the linoleum
flat with your substantial feet
and singing till the aluminum hums
and even the cabinets applaud,
you show me again beyond saying
the figure a poem should make.

9. *Benediction*

Believe me, Belinda: I never thought
Everything could be so charged with you.
Like yesterday: the slow-climbing bubble
In a tilted honey jar reminded me
Not of my father's level, but of you.
Doesn't that seem peculiar? It's
As if we've left our likeness everywhere,

As if, on any night, when we finally
Nest in bed, curled to our legs' kindling, there's
Nothing beyond our breathing: the fire is banked.
Everything else is a dream you rise to tell.

GILBERT WHITE AND THE BOBWHITE

In bed, I read,
   The language of birds
     is very ancient, and like other

ancient modes
   of speech, very elliptical;
     little is said, but much is meant

and understood.
   I marked the book, *The*
     Natural History of Selbourne,

and listened.
   I heard an early bird,
     lungful of light in the ash,

preaching beans
   into their green canoes,
     calling his fallen congregation

to *repent, restore,*
   measuring the whole notes
     over and over, plain as weather,

until diminished trees re-
   member themselves, wrenching
      trim limbs and lumbersome trunks

through painted knobs
   and knots and rotten stumps
      and generations of deadwood, spreading

a dense genealogy
   underground, dark mirror
      of the clear air's plentitude.

I rose to claim
   the world the bird and I
      had restored, but saw instead

a jay's blue cursive
   disappear into the branches
      and bray the bright throat away,

as instantly
   blades and needles
      seemed to return to rust

and the dying elm,
   no real leaves left to flame,
      showered down its sap on the dry walk.

SUMMER MODES

1.

Bluebird on the beanpole
loitering, aimless beauty!

until a cabbage moth wobbles
across the garden like an idea

and the bird swoops to it
sharp as a shard of sky.

2.

Swallows sweep
overhead at dusk

faster than chatter
in phone wires,

swerve away
in deft non sequitur

to take another
insect aside.

VISITING CAPE HATTERAS

Down to the last
windy sliver of dune, the final
blue pulse ashore,

one might persist,
for a while, in merely seeing
beach, sea, or *sky,*

despite protean
diversions—ocean's instant ridges
shellacking a range

mountain-perfect
flat on the slope of shore, or later
as light tides out

on the dark road
home, a sudden mapblue sky and loud
outer bank of clouds.

REFLECTIONS FROM THE OUTER BANKS

The egret bent to his image
stalks the shallows,
skates forward so gingerly
fish ignore his comic legs, his beak
that forks them like lightning.

Is every poem, necessarily,
about poetry?

Flickering like the fish-cloud
suspended just below surface,
a fleet of whitecap terns
treads air, waits for that sudden flash,
that initial breach
to trigger kamikaze dives.

Must poems press the world to show
what we already know?

Huge wings sweep over
smooth as memory on its well-oiled hinge,
precisely tangent to wavetip—
the black skimmer with his beak
scissoring the surf,
the pelican before he angles,
perfect arrow, into profound water.

Do poems preserve things from decay
or eviscerate, fillet?

PISGAH BALD

Birds of praise, bees abloom
in the laurel slick, butterflies
blowing upslope and away—

easy to imagine the far ridge
lofty and possible, crowned with
the rhododendrons' royal air:

the mountains, old chameleons,
offer their best pitch, hinting
bird's-eye view, only to leave you

crested and thicketed and still
surrounded, the tin roofs and silos
flashing in the valley like signals.

SHENANDOAH

Flurries of dogwood, fields clouded with cows,
Floridians climbing the slopes slower than spring:
time thins with air, whole hours suspended
perfect as birds gliding the wind's high ridge,
the blue earth's turning speed enough. Whole days

condense to a moment: the flame azaleas
and cardinals, the soft green curtain ridge
pleated between peaks, the vanishing points
soundless again under the sky's bright tiding
and remote as the blue relief of the heart.

PLAIN AIR

How hard to take the trail
as it comes, digressive,
narrow-minded with underbrush
or switchbacks, to expect
anything other than risers
of root and rock, brook and sky
retreating like careful animals.

How hard to settle for less
than luxurious prospect,
a log in a small clearing
quick with insects and curious
weeds, the song of descent
short, flat, blunt, never
hammered into a dulcimer form.

About the Author

Michael McFee was born in Asheville, North
Carolina, and educated at the University of North Car-
olina at Chapel Hill, where he was poetry editor
of the *Carolina Quarterly* from 1977 to 1979. He won the
Discovery/*The Nation* award in 1980 and a Push-
cart Prize for 1981–82. His poems have appeared widely
and his essays have been published in *Parnassus:
Poetry in Review, Chicago Review,* and elsewhere. A mem-
ber of the National Book Critics Circle, he now
lives in Durham, North Carolina.

photo by Belinda A.P. McFee

University Presses of Florida, the agency of the
State of Florida's university system for publication of
scholarly and creative works, operates under
policies adopted by the Board of Regents. Its offices are
located at 15 Northwest 15th Street, Gainesville,
Florida 32603.

Library of Congress Cataloging in Publication Data
McFee, Michael
  Plain air

  (University of Central Florida contemporary po-
etry series)
I. Title. II. Series.
PS 3563.C3634P5   1983   811'.54   83-9109
ISBN 0-8130-0774-7